C P9-BXZ-783
743.4
Learn
Donation $8

Learn to DRAW People

Copyright © 2016 by Racehorse for Young Readers

All rights reserved. No part of this book may be reproduced in any manner without the express written consent of the publisher, except in the case of brief excerpts in critical reviews or articles. All inquiries should be addressed to Racehorse Publishing, 307 West 36th Street, 11th Floor, New York, NY 10018.

Racehorse for Young Readers books may be purchased in bulk at special discounts for sales promotion, corporate gifts, fund-raising, or educational purposes. Special editions can also be created to specifications. For details, contact the Special Sales Department, Skyhorse Publishing, 307 West 36th Street, 11th Floor, New York, NY 10018 or info@skyhorsepublishing.com.

Racehorse for Young Readers™ is a pending trademark of Skyhorse Publishing, Inc.®, a Delaware corporation.

Visit our website at www.skyhorsepublishing.com.

10 9 8 7 6 5 4 3 2 1

Print ISBN: 978-1-944686-25-3

Printed in China

Learn to DRAW People

How to Draw like an Artist in 5 Easy Steps

FOR YOUNG READERS

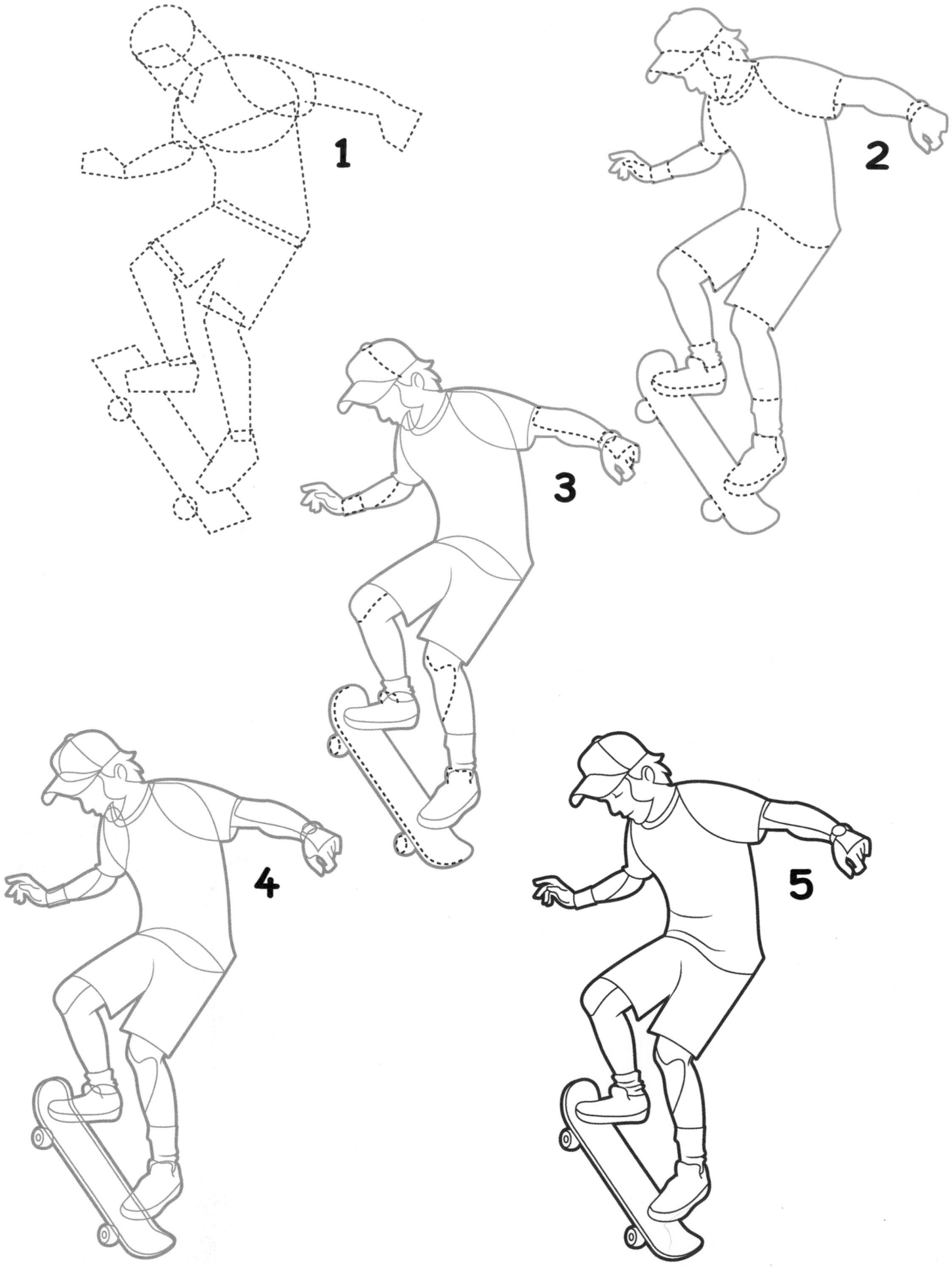
1
2
3
4
5

Practice Page

1
2
3
4
5

Practice Page

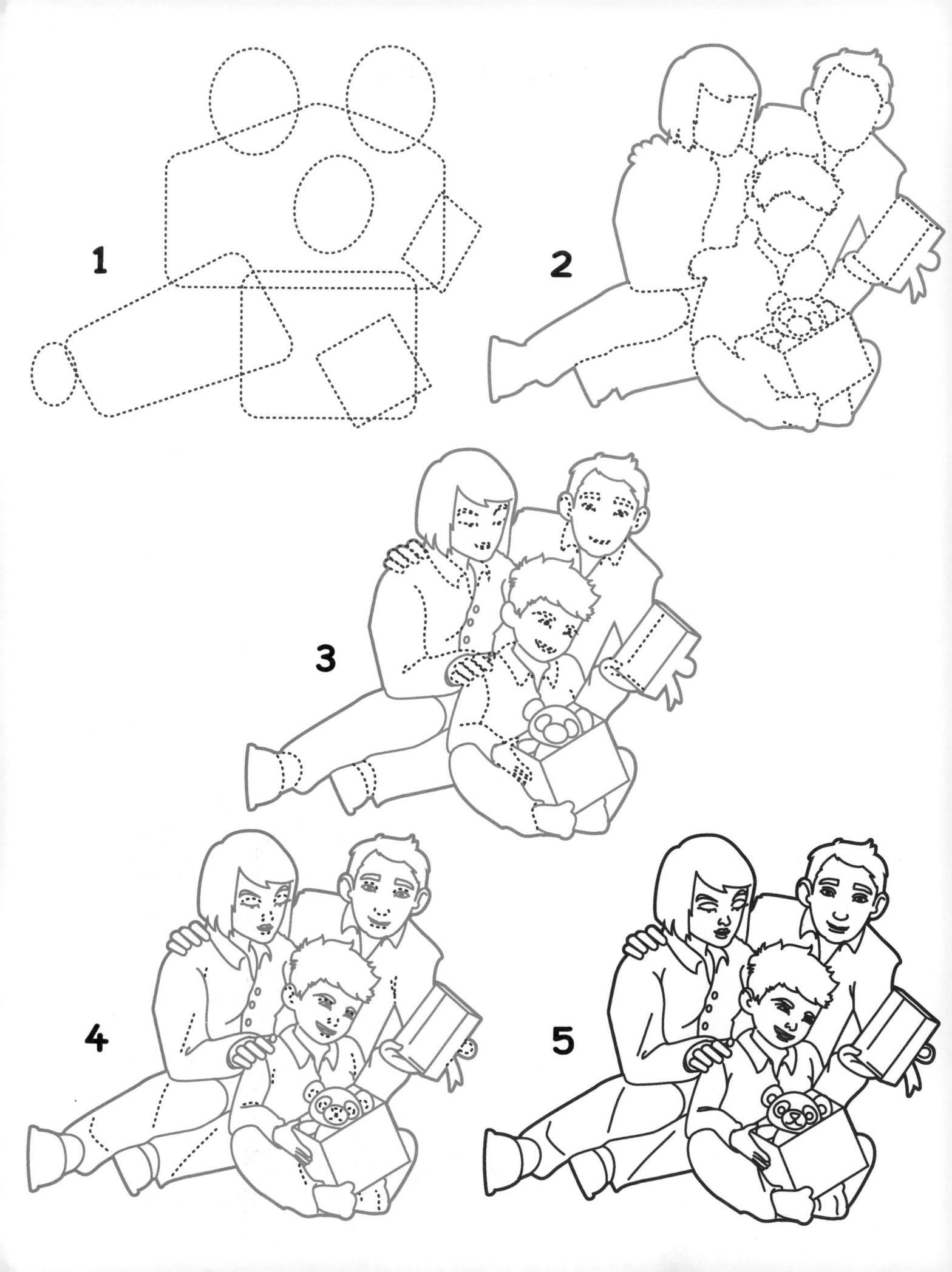
1
2
3
4
5

Practice Page

1
2
3
VET
4
VET
5
VET

Practice Page

1
2
3
4
5

Practice Page

1
2
3
4
5

Practice Page

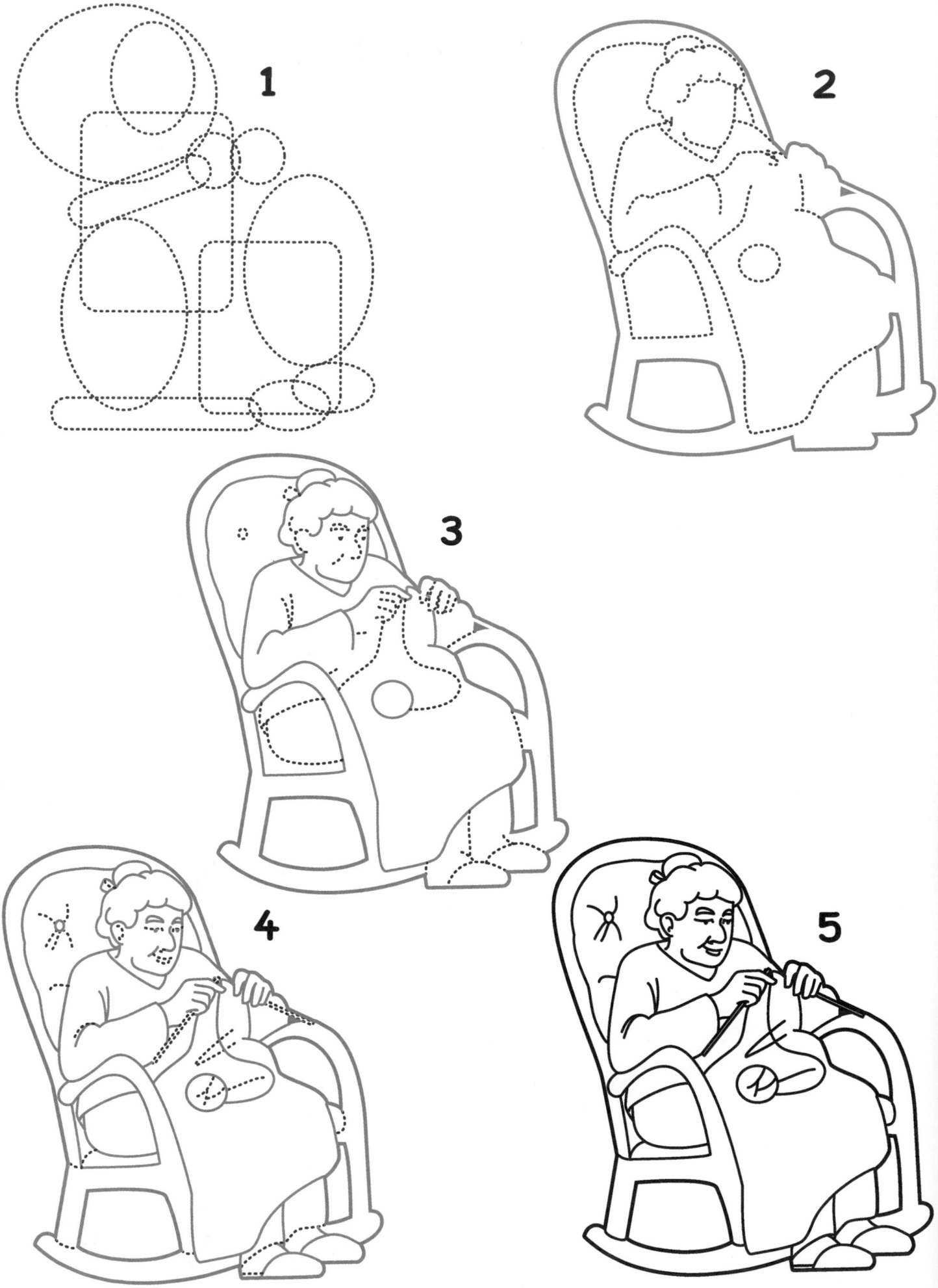
1
2
3
4
5

Practice Page

1
2
3
4
5

Practice Page

1
2
3
4
5

Practice Page

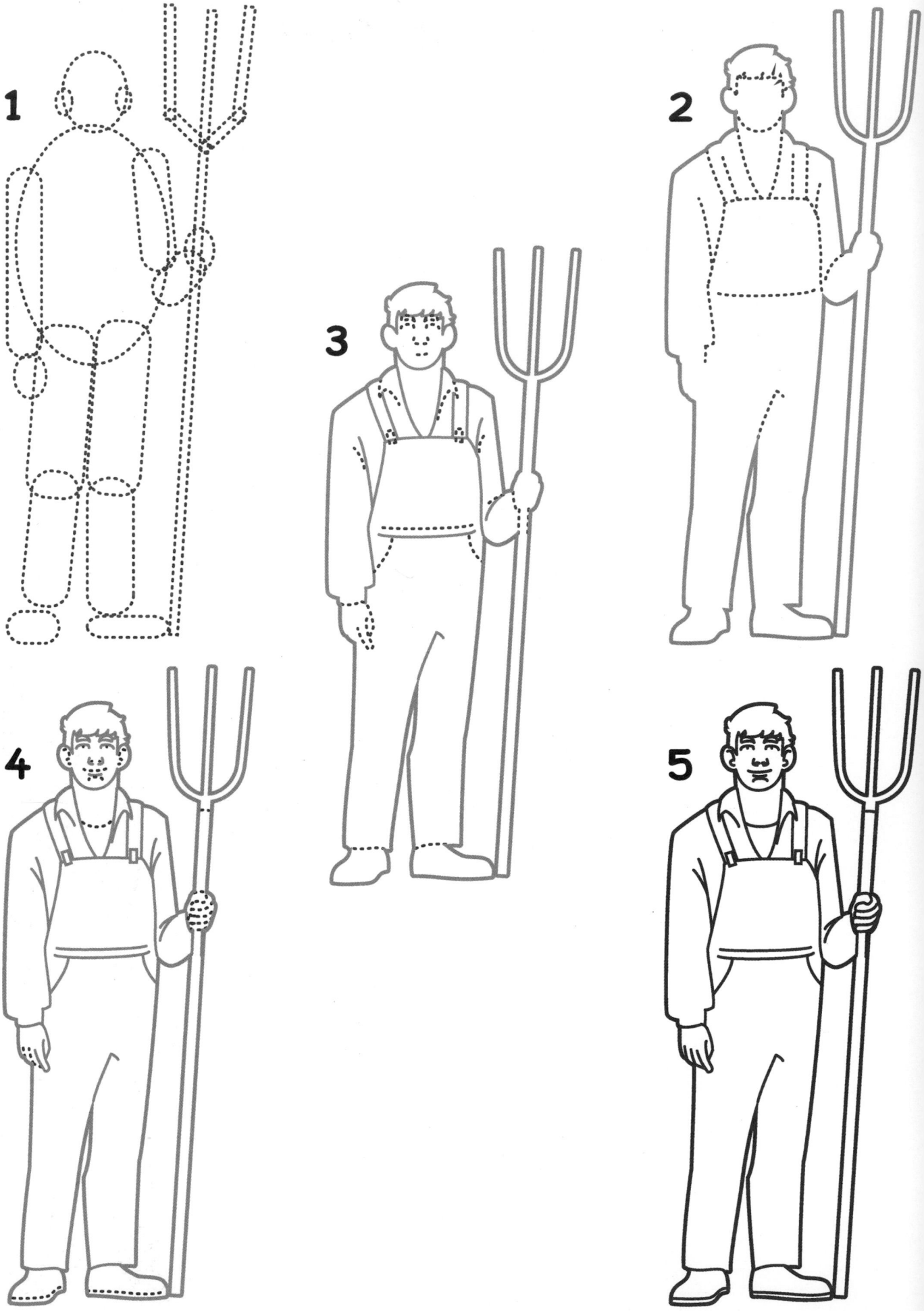
1
2
3
4
5

Practice Page

1
2
3
4
5

Practice Page

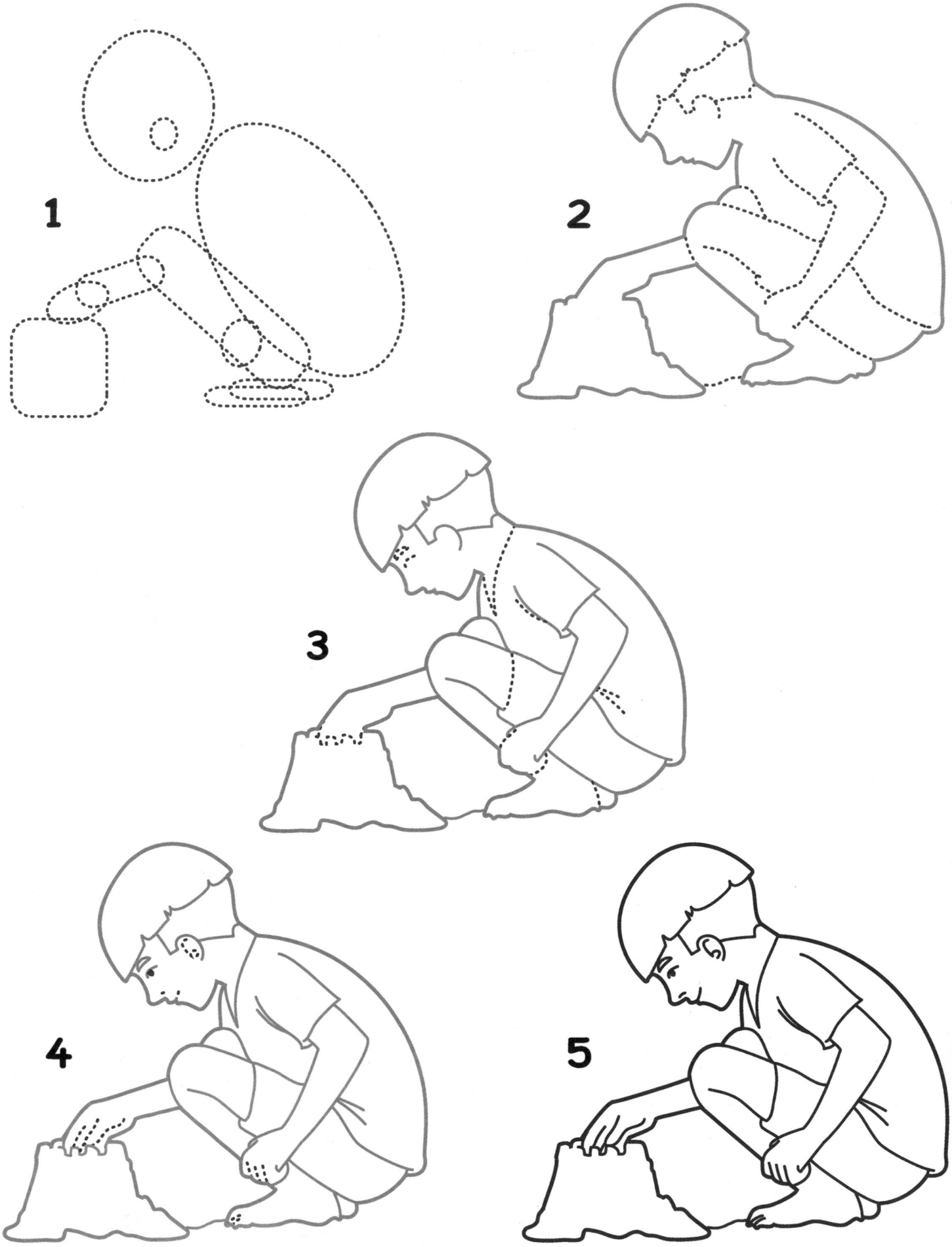
1
2
3
4
5

Practice Page

1
2
3
4
5

Practice Page

1
2
3
4
5

Practice Page

1
2
3
4
5

Practice Page

1
2
3
4
5

Practice Page

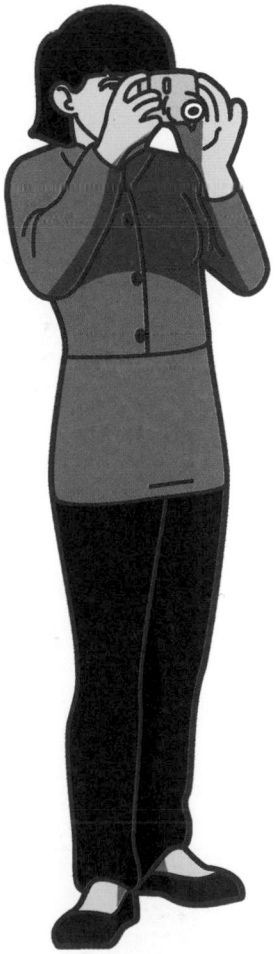

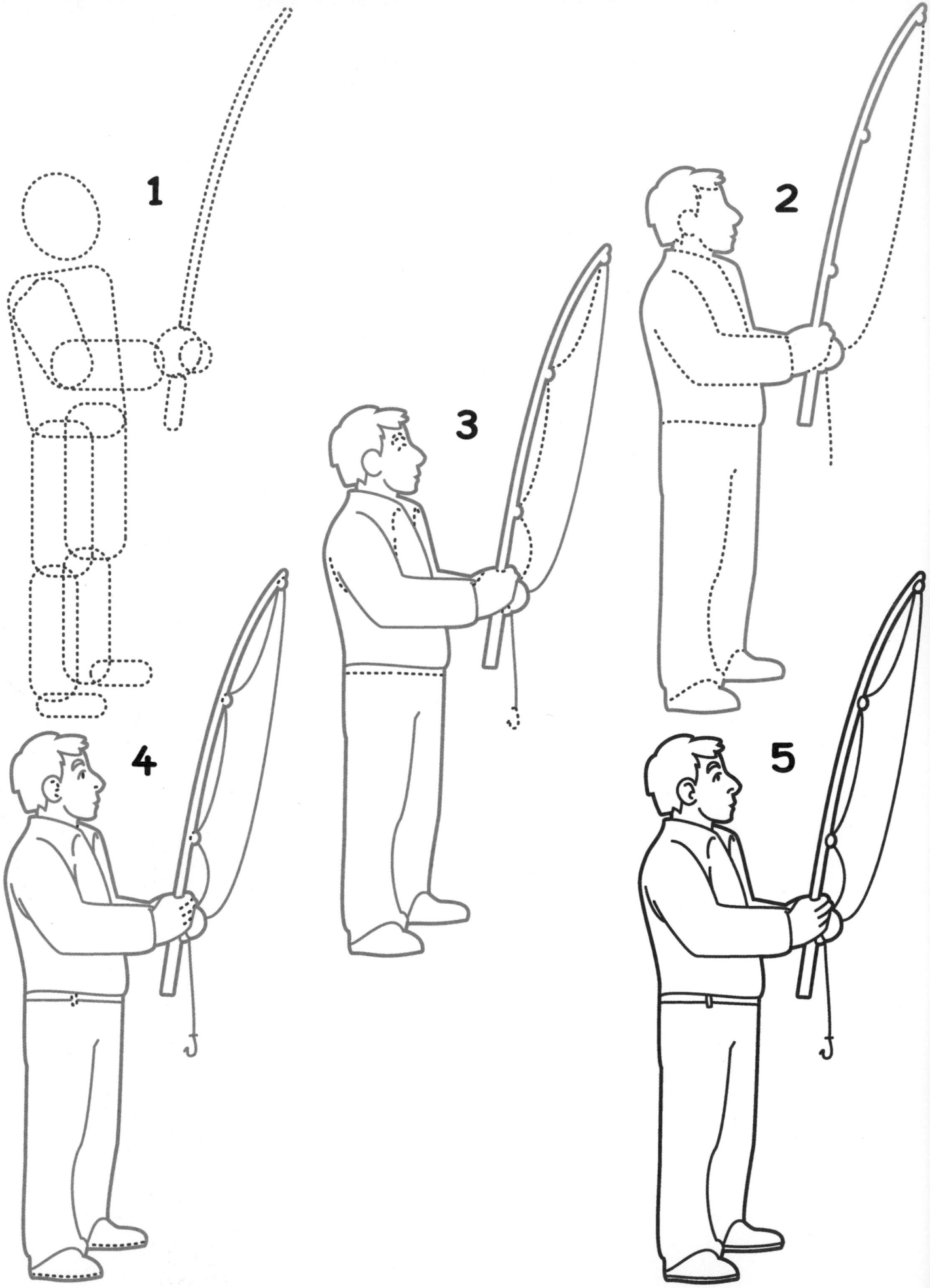
1
2
3
4
5

Practice Page

1
2
3
4
5

Practice Page

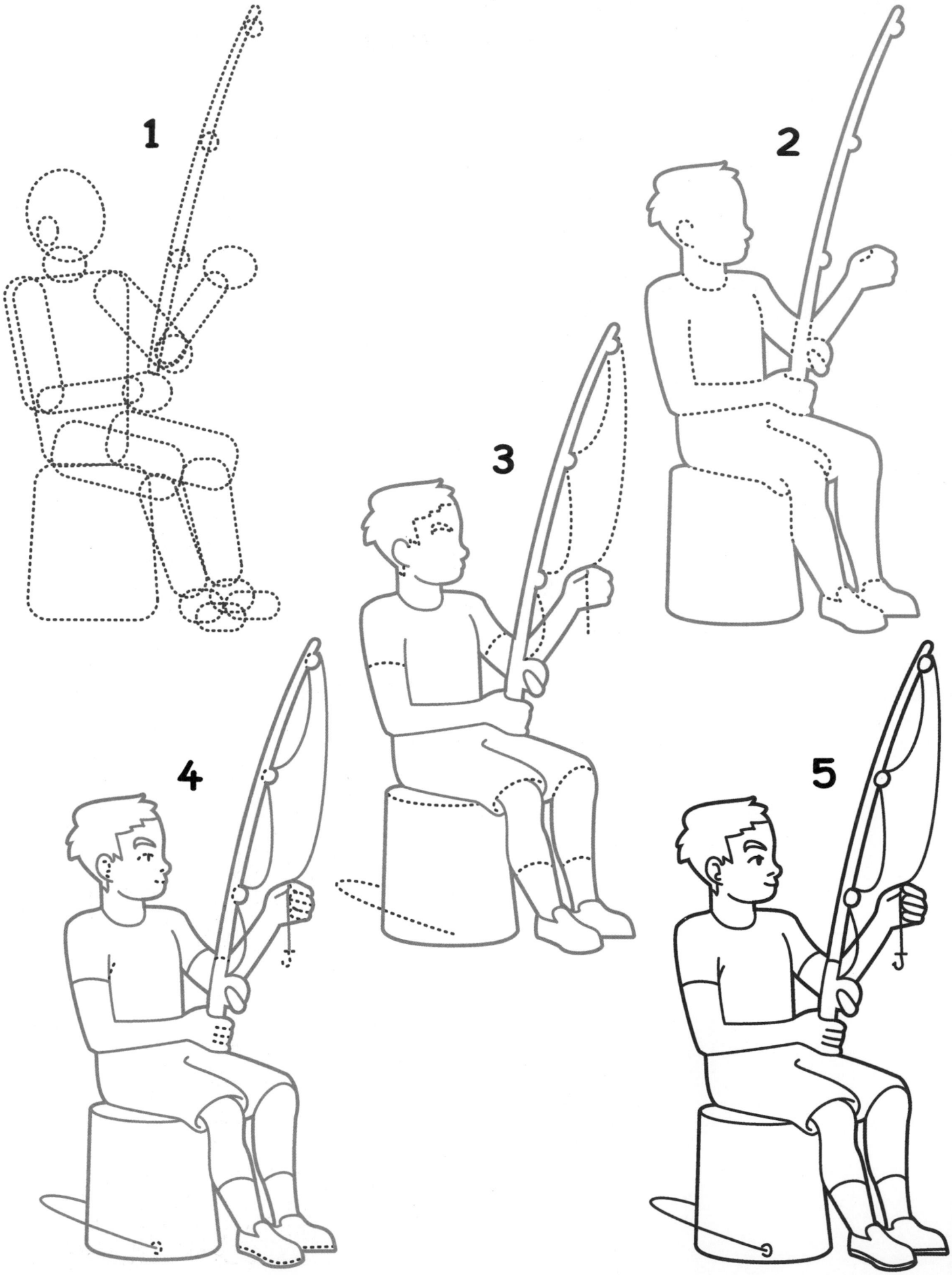
1
2
3
4
5

Practice Page

1
2
3
4
5

Practice Page

1
2
3
4
5

Practice Page

1
2
3
4
5

Practice Page

1
2
3
4
5

Practice Page

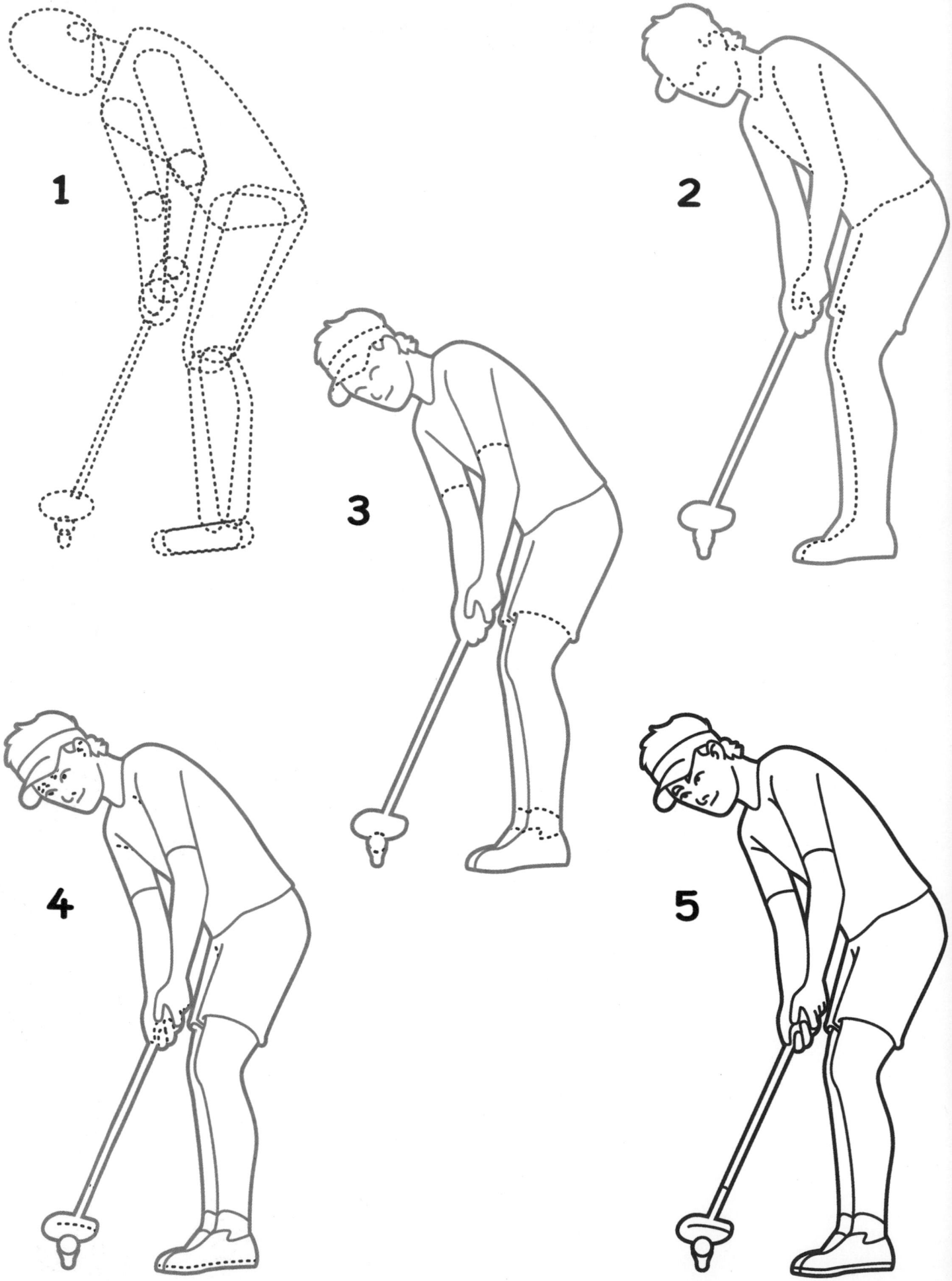
1
2
3
4
5

Practice Page

1
2
3
4
5

Practice Page

1
2
3
4
5

Practice Page

1
2
3
4
5

Practice Page

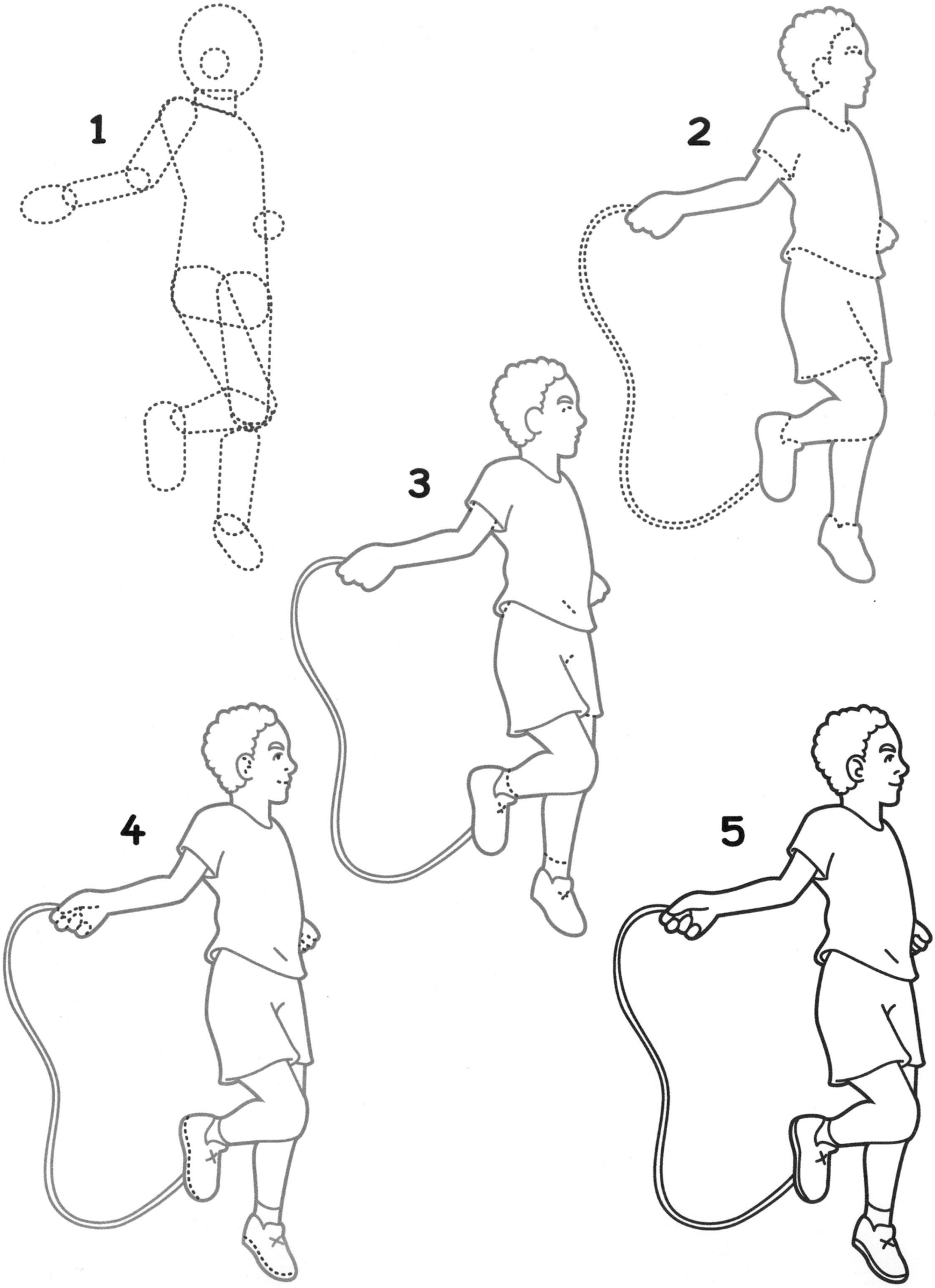
1
2
3
4
5

Practice Page

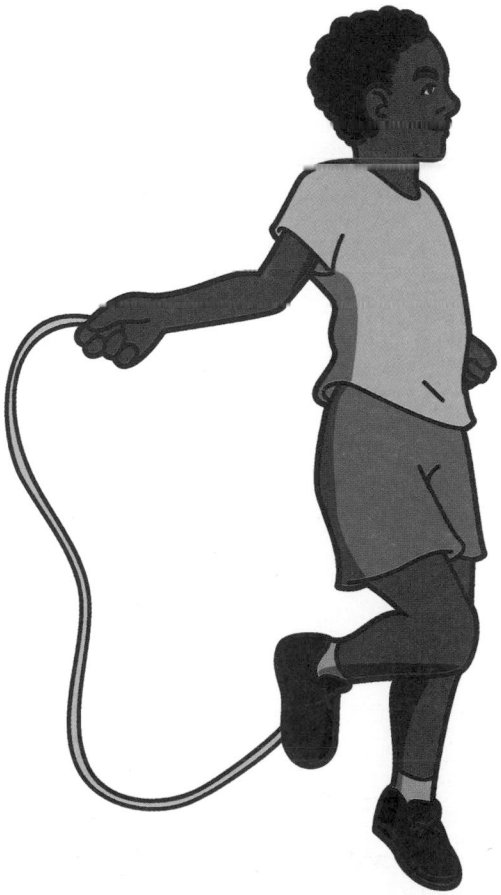

1
2
3
4
5

Practice Page

1
2
3
4
5

Practice Page

COLORING PAGES

Practice your new skills here!

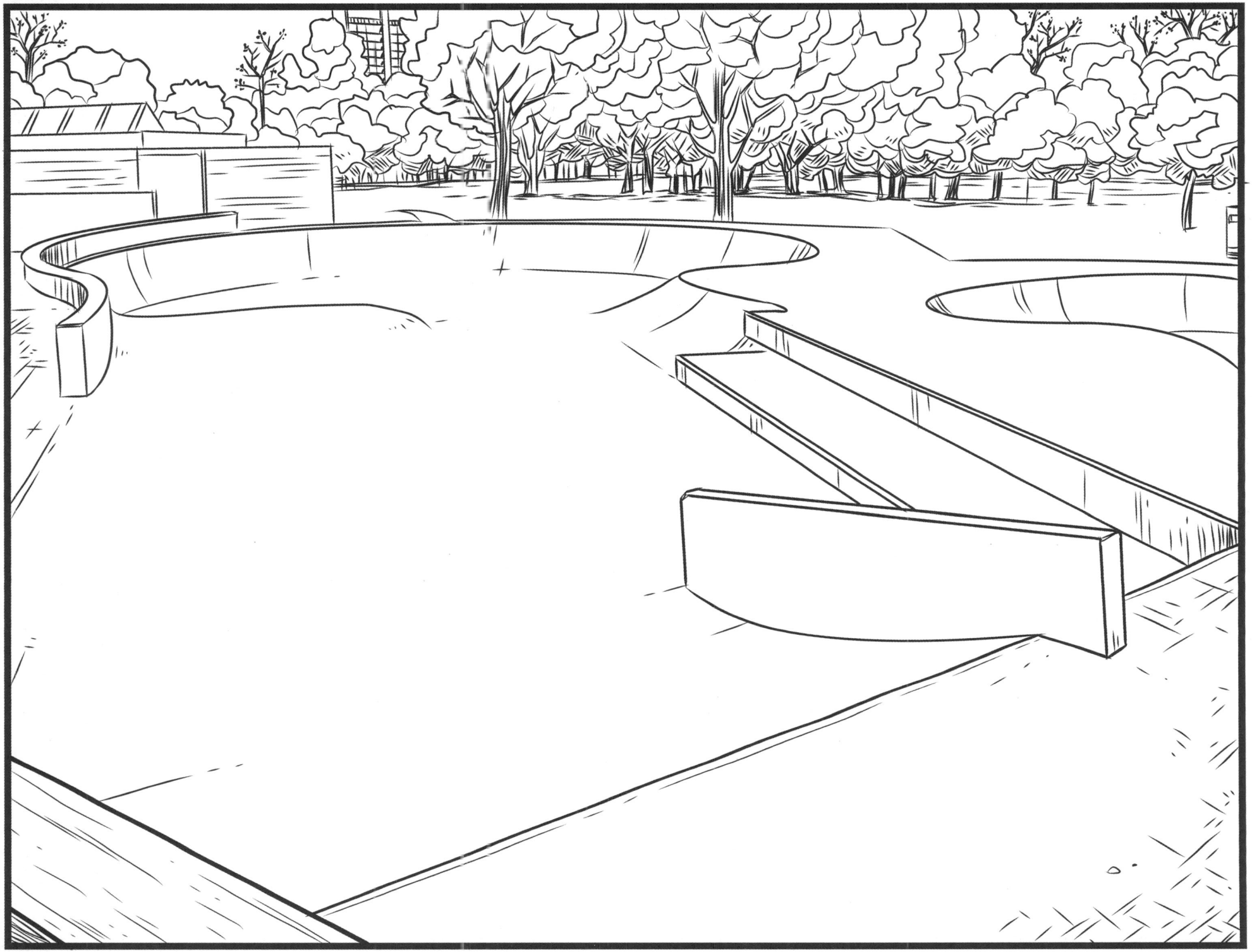